Whispers from Above

answers for a wailing heart

Felora Ziari

CRIMSON WOMAN

CRIMSON WOMAN PUBLISHING

Reviews

"When I learned it was fine to be vulnerable," writes Felora Ziari, "I gained my true strength back ... I had overcome the fear of being seen." This moving collection of poetry and prose is a testament to both vulnerability and strength. She fights for the empowerment of women and shows us all the way by finding "the nightingale in her own heart." She has written tenderly and with deep honesty about the unbearable moments as well as those that take us to the mystery of being here. Bravo.

Paula D'Arcy,
author of *Waking Up To This Day* and *Gift of the Red Bird*

The ache and joy of Spiritual wisdom cries and sings from Felora's true essence in *Whispers from Above*. Her poetry is lovingly and longingly a gift of Grace. Listen to her voice as she guides you to your own inner Truths.

Joyce Beck,
Psychotherapist and Co-founder of the Crossings

More than a book of poetry, more than a memoir, *Whispers from Above* is an exploration of the exigencies of women everywhere. From a mystical perspective it explores the restrictions that society places on women, the masks that they adopt to respond to those restrictions, and the spiritual growth that each woman must find in her own heart so that she can rise above the masks. *Whispers from Above* will change the way you look at life.

Ron Frazer,
author of *The Jacinta Joseph Caribbean Adventures, Time Branches*

Whispers from Above is a waterfall of wisdom as the author ever so gently leads us to align with our own Source of truth. This is a first book and reads as though the author is sitting across the room from you. Through eloquent language, laced with simplicity, it unveils the author's grateful journey from trials to transformation. Her beautiful transparency and exposed vulnerability draw the reader more deeply inside with each turning page. Rooted in a deep belief in a listening Presence outside of ourselves, her book invites the reader to explore a deeper level of introspection. I couldn't put it down. It's a beautiful, fluid read.

Ginger Blair,
author of *Knowing*

Whispers from Above:
answers for a wailing heart

by Felora Ziari

First Edition

Copyright © 2014 Crimson Woman Publishing

ISBN: 978-0-9906974-0-4

All rights reserved. This book or any portion thereof may not be reproduced or used in any manner whatsoever without the express written permission of the publisher except for the use of brief quotations in a book review.

For additional copies, see www.crimsonwoman.com, www.amazon.com, or your local bookseller.

DEDICATION

This book is in memory of my beloved father, Jahangir Assadi Ziari, who taught me the meaning of love and compassion. He embodied humility—a humility I am ever searching for in myself. Deeply dedicated to "service," my father took great pains to connect hearts to the Divine. He believed in the essential goodness in us.

My father brought much joy and laughter into the lives of many. To this day, family and friends remember him for his keen humor and more than anything else, we remember a gentle man and the profound impact he made on our souls.

TABLE OF CONTENTS

Introduction 1
- Hold Me in Grace 3

Search within 9
- Let Me Believe 13
- The Missing Link 17
- Self-Appointed Guardian 21
- The Broken Voice 23
- Awakening 25

Overcoming 27
- Author of My Destiny 31
- Ancestral Love 35
- Deliver Me 37
- True Power 39
- Honor Me, Honor Me 41
- Cup of Insight 45
- A Quest to Conquer Fears 47
- See My Soul 51

Faith 55
- A Cry in the Throat of the Bird of Truth 59
- Unwavering Faith 63
- Finding Yourself 65
- Greatest Expression 67

The life I left behind 69
- Memory 73
- The Heart of the Village 79
- Naneh-Joon 85
- Grapevine Tree 87
- Don't Let Go of My Hand 93

Dreaming the dream 97
- Best Friend 102
- The Mask of the Lion 106
- A Clearing Dream 110

A woman's voice: a journey to inner beauty....114
    Voice of Truth..118
    The Whispering Angel..120
    Solace of the Eyes...124
    Do You Hear My Voice?...128

ABOUT THE AUTHOR...131

Credits...134

Introduction

*"When your heart surrenders to the divine in you,
your inner poetry will shimmer."*

— Felora Ziari

Hold Me in Grace

A clenched heart
Displayed at the altar
At the dusk of all past memories,
A pearl within come to life.
I cry out to be held in grace,
Looked upon as an ornament of truth.

Begging for mercy, a hopeless place,
To be embraced in compassion, my cry,
Time moves on, but the hour stays.
Memories pass, but pain persists.
To what end are my cries held within?
Departing from this moment, my desire!

Hold me in grace, I cry.
Hold me in grace, so I dwell in forever
If forever was held in grace,
Would there ever be pain?

Memories are burdens
To the clenched heart.
In present all you can Be.
In truth you wake up.
In deceit you give up.

Hold me in Grace, I say.
Hold me in Grace.

ೞ

All of us have a *sui generis*, a unique characteristic which, when freely expressed, becomes our own magical song. Always present within each of our songs are the universal notes of Love and Grace. However, we can only witness our true self and hear our own song when our inner being is completely open to all possibilities. Then we can finally see the Truth the Sufi's call: *From the Heart's Eyes*.

Overcoming the fear of showing my authentic self is the greatest gift of my life thus far. This fear led me to distort my concept of who I was. On this journey, my self-deceptions were unveiled; thereby releasing the truest form of "me" I could know. It was as if I was learning to breathe anew, and to speak a new language. With my newly-found truest essence, I could finally hear the unique and magical song of my heart.

As we unfold as adults, our familiar childhood identity is slowly replaced with the new realities of adult life. In this new creation, we add an aspect of denial in order to survive and be accepted. My own life was no exception. It was a map of obstacles, turmoil, and victories. And each time I passed through one of these challenges, I would encounter a shift. With each shift, I gained new perspective enabling the ashes of the old version of me to give way to the emergence of my new self. Through these stages I also lost parts of me, and they were replaced with fear and self-deception.

Grief became a form of joy. It shook my inner silence. It gave a voice to the voiceless emotions inside me that I never knew existed. The challenges of life I experienced allowed me to examine the truth behind my belief systems. Was I being authentic to my own core truth, or was I merely a follower of someone else's truth? I had to question my own questions. By changing my perception, and discerning the true meaning of Truth, my life felt more aligned with the divine purpose, and the lens through which I saw this new life changed with it. My former lenses of judgments and unreal expectations gave way, and the new lens was clear. I could see Truth, a Truth which can never be divided, and one that allowed me to find freedom. Now, I saw everything was connected. I could see that every action rested upon the shoulder of another. I saw the life energy that unified us all. I was not alone anymore but lived within the Truth of Love. Now that energy was rekindled as I accepted my reality. My perception of this never fading love energy became my path to discerning the truth. Gratitude for my former life came with this grace.

Before my awakening to the Truth, I was held in a place of disbelief. My self-worth was based on the perceptions of others. My faith was not strong enough to rely on God to be my ultimate judge. With my new clarity, I desired only to live in a state of "Awe" to the fullness and beauty of life. I needed no witness to my journey.

With this new insight, I surrendered to my destiny. My poetry became my magical song and a gift of healing. I could transcend the stories I previously told myself and with this, my heart was ripped open. My poems were a cry of deliverance and transformation. With their creation I became completely present to my life. In each moment I make a conscious choice as to what my mind, heart, and spirit will witness.

I realized that, in each moment, an invisible thread of faith connects our words and thoughts with our actions. To live an enlightened life, I learned to immerse myself in the joy of life by being aware of the gap between my thoughts and actions. A gap I call the "silence of being." In this gap we can hear the words of the heart calling us to more presence in our life.

There is no discovery of self,
Only remembering who we are!

-Felora Ziari

Underneath all our struggles is the desire to discover our identity, our true nature and our purpose. For the longest time, I considered myself a seeker of Truth. I discovered, however, that I had only been seeking happiness. It hadn't yet occurred to me that happiness was transitory and would not bring me lasting joy. As I began to see life more realistically, I discerned that how I saw the external world was a mirror of how I saw myself.

Even though I thought I understood the meaning of life and my purpose, I lacked the true understanding of living a life with detachment. I realized that my challenge in finding the true meaning of detachment was my lack of trust in God's will. In the words of a Zen master, "True spiritual practice is not founded on attainment or on the miraculous, but on seeing life itself as a true miracle." True miracles only happen when we have faith and trust in the Ultimate Wisdom and remembrance of who we are. In the Four Noble Truths, the origin of suffering is attributed to attachment to transient things and the ignorance thereof.

What inspired me to search within was the day my father transitioned. On one hand, my world collapsed and I felt an unbearable pain, and, on the other, I felt an immense love for my newborn baby. How could I be in such pain and feel my life is over after the loss of my father, and, at the same time, feel exhilarated from the precious love for a new life? That day, I sat beside my son sobbing and asking for God's forgiveness for not understanding the mystery of life and abundance of love.

During a meditation at a women's retreat, everyone was asked to meditate upon the importance of bringing the gift of service and meaning to our work. The quote read, "God willing, thou mayest accomplish a deed whose fragrance shall endure as long as the Names of God… will endure."[1] During this particular reflection, I had the most amazing vision that deepened my understanding of how each of us can impact the world around us. During the meditative state, I saw myself standing in the middle of a huge arena surrounded by circles of water fountains. At first I saw water coming out of one circle of the water fountains reaching almost my height. Then I saw that the impact of the fountains created a second circle of fountains with a greater strength than the first one, and the water was zooming up higher. More and more concentric circles of fountains appeared around me. I was standing in the middle and was in awe of how I was able to see the creation of the magnificent beauty that was surrounding me. As I stood there I saw myself as the source of the water, and that each of us is a center which can influence and impact the lives of others through our deeds and servitude. Each of us could be a source of beautiful energy impacting the creation of other sources of energy. After that vision, it didn't matter how small or big my contribution was to the world, I knew it was my duty to be a fountain.

---

[1] Quote by Bahá'u'lláh

Let Me Believe

How could I have known
what the hands of destiny wrought?
Where would I have learned the games of life?
How could I have known the truth?
Is wisdom gained,
or known from the beginning of time?
Does it matter where the journey ends?

Were the gifts You gave me a token of love,
Or a test of my strength?
Was the paved road a bait
to lure me in on this rocky journey?
Are You in my heart,
Or the heart of the heartless?

How can I see the bliss
written from the time immemorial?
How can I mend the mirrored image
broken by the pebbles of deceit?
How can my drunken heart
feel the rapture of Your love?

I am looking for You
in every color in sight.
I am searching for a glimpse of Your countenance
in every grain of sand.

Let me see You in every breath
Taken in by the worthy or the infidels.

Let me fly to the apex of madness,
So I can be reminded of the world of reality.

Separate me from all the false existence in this world.
Let me gain precedence over my weak heart.
I am tired of pretending to be
what others want me to be.
Take me to the world beyond;
The promise of the Celestial World
is making me restless.
Open the gateway to the mystery of contentment!

I do not want to belong to the world of matter;
Let me leave this empty shell.
You gave me life and life is taking it away.
Let me leave this nether world so I can see.
Let me witness the Beauty You promised.
Let me breathe in the soul of air infused
with the perfume of Your love.

Let me transcend all the stories I told myself,
So I can come face to face with destiny.
Let me ride the boat of life tenderly.
Let the sail take me on a journey of faith.
Let me believe I will be taken care of.
Let me believe …
Let me believe …

ॐ

My grandmother was an inspiring woman. Even though she never went to school and could neither read nor write, she had great wisdom for understanding life. Whenever we would repeat how someone's action or word has hurt us, her response was: "You will not feel better by scratching the old wound."

The Missing Link

Pouring oil on dying fire ignites the flame.
Scratching old wounds intensifies the pain.
Exaggerating lies refutes the unspoken truth.

Deceit clothed in a garment of pretenses,
Holds us captive.
Story of an uncharted life,
Allures our heart.
Yearning to explore unfamiliar territories,
Ignites endearing excitement.

Sleepless nights,
We imagine the mystery of veiled Beauty,
Endless desire for more,
The hidden gems yet to be found.

Pouring oil on the flame of desire,
Exaggerates the beauty to be held.
The pursuit for unknown treasure,
Is a journey of discovery,
A story of human hearts,
And a never-ending search
For understanding.

In this madness,
We find a glimpse of that unknown treasure.
We realize the joy in the midst of turmoil.
The joy, transitory,

Remains in the past, a memory forgotten.
We still wake up to feel the pain,
From scratching of old wounds.
A short lived euphoria.

When this fleeting joy dies,
We open our eyes and perceive,
With a knowing heart!
The allure of a carnal life is a mirage,
An ephemeral,
Seduction of our heart.

With new insight,
We witness the wonder of the gem within.
A knowing from hearts of heart,
Without change of essence, life remains the same.
The Beauty does not lie without.

If our will is
Surrendered,
The missing link will be found.
A lover of Light within!

ଓ

Self-Appointed Guardian

Unraveling the habitation of the mind,
Drawing closer to the hem of life,
Crying for the unknown mystery,
Living for the ultimate peace,
Herein lies the hidden agenda of life.

Born of desires and wishes,
Searching for meaning,
In the tangled vine garden of our mind,
River of life pushes us forward,
Opening a pathway in the midst of confusion,
So we can explore the land of our soul.

Images of mystery form in our mind;
We become the self-appointed guardian.
We stand at the edge of the garden of our inner being,
Fearful of what could unravel.
We hesitate to partake in the mystery,
But the warmth of the sun beckons us to enter.

Dreaming of a day that will never fade,
Everlasting glory in moments of awareness,
We enter to unravel the Unknown.
Dressed in each rose, tulip, thorn and beyond,
We enter to witness the essence of Love,
Wrapped in our fear, courage, fortitude,
And in our humanness.

ॐ

The Broken Voice

Oh Mystical Angel!
Hear this broken voice,
Oblivious of unknown yearnings,
Longing to endure all in a quest
to be immersed in a state of awe,
A desire to speak with utter clarity,
And hear the music of the unheard song.

Wishing to dream the dreams
of forefathers for freedom of spirit,
Hoping to appease the unyielding desires,
Releasing the attachment to unattained aspirations.

Oh despairing voice, the response is heard.
Whisper your desires in My ears,
So I can hear the melodies of your inner longing.
Let Me heal the lamentation of your heart.
Let Me grasp the hopes tarnished in utter desperation.
To heal the sickness of your heart,
In search of wonderment,
Fix your gaze on the horizon
of fortitude and humility,
So the thirst for abounding Love
can leap forward delightfully,
In the quest for the golden crown of the Mystery ...

 CB

Awakening

An expression of life,
A celestial union,
Revelation,
Encountering one another.

You experience from my presence,
A hint of truth.
Truth mixed with expectations,
Ego and essence.

In your presence,
I fathom the depth of my spirit.
Favoring the affirmations
of my true nature.

In my presence,
Your awareness is of inner judgments.
Mirroring forth emotions,
Birthed from your attributes.

In the experience we create,
Linked with Transcendent Awareness,
You become rich in you.
And I become rich in me.
A revelation,
A mystical encounter.

ഗ

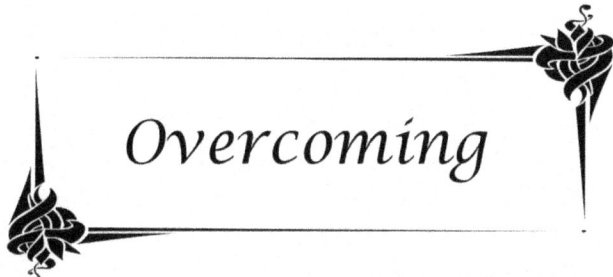

Overcoming

A Search for Truth.
To have the courage to say yes
To the unknown.
Letting go of fears.
To show up naked
In a longing to be true to our soul.

-Felora Ziari

Overcoming is the wisdom of letting go, stripping the old, climbing a mountain too hard to climb, hearing the sound of life with your inner ears and listening to the longing of your soul.

When I learned that it was fine to be vulnerable, I gained my true strength back. I showed up with all of me. I felt freedom from all the self-imposed obligations. I had overcome the fear of being seen.

As a child, I always imagined that people's personas had two sides. I knew there was a story within them that they were holding onto and did not want anyone to see. There was disharmony between their inner world and outer world. I would always listen intently to adults to see if I could hear between the lines. I was fascinated with the stories that they were not telling me. Growing up, my mother would make sure we said our daily prayers before breakfast. We would go to a private room to say our prayers. My mother would insist that we chant our prayers loud enough that she could hear them from the next room. She told us, "Chant from the depth of your heart, so God can hear your prayers, but most importantly, so God could feel your prayers." One morning, as I sat down to say my prayer, I closed my eyes and remembered my mother's remarks. It became clear to me that it didn't matter that I didn't know people's stories, what mattered was that I felt their heart.

As I got older, I knew that in order to feel free, I must let others see my inner story. I had to overcome the fear of being seen. In my desire to be accepted and loved, I closed myself to others. I had to be vulnerable, raw and exposed. Only by letting go was I to gain my true strength back. I showed up with all of me. I let God feel my prayers – not just hear them, and I felt freedom.

Author of My Destiny

When my heart crumbles in pain,
When disappointments churn the hurt,
When my face is red from the slapping hands of fate,
When no one wipes off my tears,
I forget the Author of my destiny.

When my heart clinches from fears of the unknown,
When I hear the melodies of the forbidden symphony,
When I see storms in a cloudless sky,
When I cannot feel the agonizing sighs of strangers,
I forget the Author of my destiny.

When I sleep with my eyes open
for fear of my own dreams,
When the remembrance of all that lies ahead
seems petty,
When the joy of loud laughter is a distant memory,
When I stop yearning for my Beloved,
I forget the Author of my destiny.

When the melody of the spring showers goes
unheard,
When the morning breeze does not sing my song,
When the sound of silence vibrates notes of fear,
When the warmth of the sun
sends chills through my body,
I forget the Author of my destiny.

In a world filled with fears and deception,
In the darkest hours of night,
On a reckless journey of hate and envy,
Aimlessly on a quest,
Seeking transcendent awareness,
To see the wonders of the world with naked eyes,
To behold the magnificent beauty of raw laughter,
To write a poem for the Eternal,
To taste the first drop of rain after the draught on my tongue,
Guided to the flame of the light of sublime Truth.

Life in its agonizing moments
is a journey of hopelessness,
And the mystery of blessings are concealed,
To protect us from our humanness,
To teach us faith is a gift for the chosen ones,
Bestowed as a token of Love,
From the Author of our destiny.

In this place, "I am that I am."
I see the beauty of the thorn in my soul.
I feel the warmth of love in coldness of heart,
Immersed in the storm,
I sail on a journey of gratitude,
Because "I am that …"
A witness to the Author of my destiny …

૦ૅ

Ancestral Love

The voice of my ancestors echoes,
Calling my name.
"Be true to what has been.
Generations believed so you could be."

I hear grandmother tell me,
"Child, throw your words into the well,
So it would be the repository of your words."

My grandfather points upward,
"In Him, you uphold your integrity."

My sweet aunt smiles;
Her eyes tell me all I need to know.

I hear my beloved father saying,
"My sweet daughter, show courage and have faith,
Don't forget your innocence."

"All has been, so you could become."
"The thread runs through the fabric of each soul,"
They tell me.
"All you are, and all you will become,
is the work of generations gone before."
"Open your heart, you will see."

ॐ

Deliver Me...

Deliver me from cleverness.
If intelligence is the gift
bestowed upon the brow of the worthy,
Set me free to be unworthy.
If cleverness is the culmination
of the gifted few,
Let me lament in my unworthiness.

Deliver me from cleverness,
and give me freedom,
to set my feet upon the land of humility.
To be humble in unworthiness is my wish.
To be humble in cleverness is Your desire.
Let me live in Your desire
and set me free from my wish.

ଓ

True Power

Sometimes, we sing the song of love
With anger in our heart,
And sometimes we chant prayers of gratitude
With revenge in our mind.
Sometimes our light shines in the spring
And sometimes our shadow is cast in the fall.

When faith is an illusion of truth,
It comes in many shades,
A sense of false power,
Wrapped in a shroud of immortality.
Duality of essence,
Reality masked,
Evading the Truth.

We say we have faith,
But in reality,
We choose the faith we have.

For an enlightened heart,
Love and dismay cannot dwell in one abode.
Deliverance is to honor the obstacles in our journey,
And our gratitude for pain
Allows the covenant to unlock
The oracle of a veiled mystery.
Where we could marvel the wonderment,
Letting our shadow swim away
In the river of life's mystery,
We are drowned in Light.

ೞ

Honor Me, Honor Me

The bird of Love roaming amongst the tulips,
Bursting from the inner chamber
of knowledge of God,
Yearning for immense gratitude,
Singing the melody of patience.

"Honor Me! Honor Me!"
The cry is heard.
To you I am only a journey.
A journey that leads to happiness and joy,
A path to contentment in the mortal world,
Granting wishes hidden in your heart.

"Honor Me! Honor Me!"
With gratitude,
And discern My true Essence,
An Essence lost for generations in the clash of egos,
Lost in a battle between power and faith.
I am more than a journey
to complete the circle of life;
I am the mystery of wonderment and bliss,
Hidden in the depth of your heart,
Waiting to be awakened.

"Honor Me! Honor Me!"
By igniting the flame of devotion,
Whispering the sweet melody of rapture,
Enkindling the undying torch of sacred love,
Unfolding the Truth
hidden in the inner realm of your heart.
And, having faith that the journey never ends.

༄

Cup of Insight

The Endless desire to be right
Shapes the story
Masking the truth that hurts.
Vibrations can be heard,
And when heeded,
a journey revealed.

Life is filled with idle fancies,
Yours and mine, against reality.
In ultimate wisdom, we choose;
Not accepting wisdom has boundaries

Some desire joy, bliss.
Look for the light that hides their shadows.
Oblivious of their fragmented mind,
Find a passage to satisfy their drunken hearts.

Others, thirsty for the cup of insight,
Tear asunder the veil that holds them back,
Revealing wisdom of their choices,
Knowing desires are reflections of state of mind.

೮ಽ

A Quest to Conquer Fears

Betrayal of love tore me to pieces.
In the arena of senseless life,
I am left alone to tend to a tattered heart.
Where are the angels watching over me?

Tired of pretending, I lay my head
on the bosom of resignation,
Waking up to reality of indignation,
Surrendering to the prison of self,
Where are the mystical guardians holding my hands?

The Beloved promised I would never be left alone.
The search for belonging is pulling me astray.
The yearning for understanding
is bleeding in my heart.
Where are the spirits of hope granting my wish?

Wake me up from this dreary dream;
I am tired of searching for wonderment and meaning.
Desiring virtuous sentiment
for undeserved compassion,
Where is the surging ocean of benevolence?

Hear the sigh of this broken bird,
Tending to the wounds of the emotional taunt,
Shedding tears of irony for a choiceless path,
Where are the guiding lights leading me to safety?

Fill up the chalice of passion and desire,
So I can step out of this dark prison,
Singing bravely the melody of hope,
And hear the songs of the angels
carrying me on their shoulders.

Give me one more chance to dance with destiny,
To ignite the flame of fortitude,
To behold the unbinding deliverance from resignation,
And lay my head on the bosom of righteousness.

Give me one more chance to dance with the angels.
Give me one more chance
to sing with the mystical guardians.
Give me one more chance
to swim in the ocean of benevolence.
Give me one more chance
to conquer the fears that hold me back.
The fears that hold me back…

ಲ

See My Soul

So many a day, I cry for being a woman;
So many a day, I regret being me.

When the gift of awareness is not in hand,
Beauty becomes a curse,
Immersing those who fail to see
In lessons so hard to learn.

You looked at me and saw only flesh;
I dared you, "See my soul."
Afraid of what you barely glimpsed,
You turned away.

On some days,
I become enslaved to the "shoulds" of this world
The ties that bind me are what others want me to be.
Then on some days,
I wake and live the myth of the brave,
A lonesome woman
committed to the gift of fortitude.

Living the lies of the ego,
Holds me captive,
To hide behind the mask of the flesh.
But then,
Under the cover of deception,
My heart sobs for the wisdom
To dare to show all of me.

Is there solace
To be found amidst the confusion?
Must we turn inward,
And be in our own world?

But, bravery is to stand in the world,
Alone,
Playing the trumpet that knows the unsung melodies.
As a pioneer of sound on a journey of devotion,
Opening the canopy of the forest,
Ushering the bird within to soar,
And find the unlimited Celestial Realm,
And land in the field of freedom,
A singing witness to true nobility,
Always present.

ω

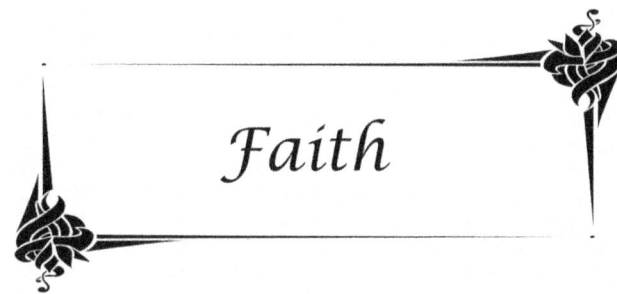

"As above, so below."
Faith is to unveil
The things I thought I knew
And the things I never knew.
Faith is to grasp the magic of life.
To truly listen to the whisper of my heart,
A witness to a deep knowing.

-Felora Ziari

Faith is to believe, to embrace life fully, to love and be open to being loved, to accept the reality that we are all connected, and are part of one divine plan. Faith is knowledge and a guiding light. Faith is also the awareness that on our quest to unravel the Mystery of life, we need to remember to live the mystery of the moment.

The treasures of Divine mystery appear in our lives in many forms. One day as I was gazing outside through the window, I saw the beauty of my surroundings in a way that I had never seen before. Everything was merged together, trees, sky, birds, wind, light and beyond. I saw the oneness of all the elements. The magnificent beauty was breathtaking. I had the realization that in our custom of naming something we diminish its true beauty by separating it from its environment. The fullness of life could not be fully recognized if we fail to see ourselves as part of the whole, if we believe we are separated from the essential unity.

By being a witness to the divine presence in everything, we can hear the whisper of our heart and grasp our true self and our calling. In the philosophy of "Ubuntu" in the African tradition a person is a person through other people. "I am who I am because of who we all are." The true essence of life can only be realized when one is part of the whole.

The whispers of our heart can also allow us to overcome the obstacles that show up in our lives. These obstacles are the creative power that leads us to expand the understanding of ourselves. In dealing with the hindrances of life, a part of us dies, giving ways for something new to emerge and blossom. In a dream, I heard my father telling me, "To understand life you need to understand death." The true meaning of death is to understand dying to oneself, unlearning things we have learned that no longer benefit us, unveiling the masks of ego, becoming detached from the transitory things of the world. The journeys of discovery to live a meaningful life are leading me to learn the meaning of True Love. When life is an illusion, as Hindu's call Maya, "that which is not," we get lost in the little tragedies of our lives and become a reflection of the world around us.

Faith is about understanding that only Love is real. Everything else—that which is not Love—separates us from God. Since the beginning, our journey as human beings has been to return to that love.

> *All knowledge is but a branch of worship and all worship is but a branch of abstinence, and all abstinence is but a branch of trust in God and trust in God has neither limit nor finite end.*
>
> - M a k k i

A Cry in the Throat of the Bird of Truth

Will a myriad of knowledge fathom life?
Will ignited fire of love bound the desire?

Beneath the thunder of lingering pain,
Dreamers wither in the fire of naked truth.
Masking the reality, permitting deceit,
Fearing the Friend, protecting the veil,
Yellow leaves falling off
in the autumn wind.
Dwellers on the clouds of sky,
Reckless vapors leaving no trace,
No courage to let go of the fears.

In a quest to fathom the tale of life,
Love is the seeker's reality,
A portal to a magical journey,
Leaving the mortal claim
To grasp the beauty of the song
of yearnings of the human heart;
Remembering the Decree
To wipe the dust off the mirror of the heart,
And write on its cradle,
The melody of the Spirit.

Gaining hundreds of lives,
Is the martyrs wisdom,
Paving the path of fortitude,
Forgetting the past.

Delighted is he who has witnessed!
Delighted is he who has believed!
Passing the gift of love
To heal the wounds,
Leading the journey
From dust to Light,
To become a cry
In the throat of the bird of Truth.
To become a cry
In the throat of the bird of Truth.

༃

The following poem came to me one day as I remembered a favorite saying of my grandmother, Naneh-joon: "Child, in life you need courage! Just like the tree, the wind of life will shake you every so often to test your faith."

Unwavering Faith

Is there a tree that the wind did not tremble?
Is there an ocean
that did not rest its head upon the shore?
Is there a heart that did not despair?
Is there a lover who did not sigh for their beloved?
Is there a mystical angel that was not heard?

Through life's endless desires and afflictions,
we journey.
We endure the wind of tribulations
To irrevocably reach the shore of acceptance.
To bow our heads to unwavering faith
In this, lies life's mystery.

ଓଃ

Finding Yourself

Your heart is My abode.
In nobility, I made you whole.
In fear, you broke into splinters.
Fear, sprouted from betrayal
of love and your reality.
The rest of your life,
you will search to "find yourself,"
To find your "life's purpose,"
Not knowing all along,
You held all the pieces in your grasp,
Never lost, needing to be found.

Keep your feet firm on My ground,
With heart filled with gratitude,
So I can take your spirit to the Celestial World,
Sweep you off the solid ground,
Mend the shattered pieces,
And open your heart to trust,
Where fear will not find a place to reside.

Greatest Expression

In the cradle of the earth,
Wandering gypsy of my heart,
Urges to be free,
Takes an oath,
"Climb Everest;
Win the heart of the mountain."

In the citadel of the world,
Blossoming victory of acceptance,
Diminish the desire for self-indulgence.
Grasp the expanse of Understanding.

A journey on the river of Faith,
Violins play in the absence of contradiction
A song of Truth.
Pride washes away in the face of humility.
Climbing fervently to reach the peak,
To release from the cage
The nightingale of my heart.

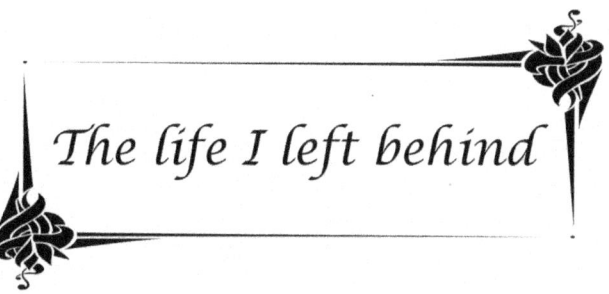

The life I left behind

I wish there was no wish
So I could always remember
The roots that gave me wings
In the bosom of the ancient wisdom.
To remember to laugh again.
To remember what I forgot "growing up".

-Felora Ziari

When I left Iran, I never imagined that it would take twenty-three years before I returned home. In my long absence, I lost my father and my grandparents and on my return the void of their absence could not be filled. With their loss, my sense of belonging to the life I knew was tainted.

When I was 10 years old, I was sitting outside on the porch at our family home watching a spring rain shower. This was the best time of the year. I loved the sound of the raindrops hitting the concrete and the smell of the dirt from the garden. I was watching the rain shower when the rain suddenly stopped and the rays of the sun illumined the beautiful garden my mom planted. I felt as if I had to understand the story of the rain and the sun.

It was as if the day was a nudge from God telling me to look for the meaning behind the veil of the dark clouds, telling me that life is a combination of the rain and the sun; it changes all the time. We go through rainstorms, but, inevitably, the sun will shine again. There is beauty in every moment. Cherishing every moment is a choice. Remembering every moment is a choice. To bear witness to the language of love in which God speaks is a choice.

As an adult, I had forgotten the moment of the spring rain, but, when I returned home after all those years, the moment was ever present in that place where I witnessed the fullness of life and where I first heard the language of God.

Memory

Wonders I have beheld.
Many lives I have lived.
Story of broken hearts.
Story of awe and wonder.
Story of defeat.
All lie within my heart.
Memories, bundle of light and shadows,
Joy and sorrows.

Childhood memories have linked,
Pieces of me back to me.
Home, after twenty-three years pass,
The place I was birthed,
Where it held the breath of my family.
I was seventeen, twenty-three years ago,
And my father was still alive.
He is lost to us now.
Family waiting at the door,
The same door I dreamed of opening.
Joy and pain merged in a knot in my heart,
Life moved on in this home,
But stood stagnant in my heart.
Memories, bundle of light and shadows,
Joy and sorrows.

On my return, that second day out with Mom,
I wore the hijab, which now was the custom,
A long overcoat and a headscarf
I wore a beautiful green chiffon shawl.

The sidewalks full of people,
Fruits, vegetables, clothes, rugs,
Shops filled with women,
Bargaining for better prices,
Satisfying their power struggle to win—
The only place where they had a chance.
Hustle, bustle, noises now unfamiliar,
Corners full of people living, living lives.

With every passerby she knew
Mom would stop, smile
And exclaim, "This is my daughter from America."
Congratulations with kisses—three now?
Cheek, cheek, and cheek again,
A new trend for me.
There must be more love, here, now.
Or must they convince each other more of that love?
I still forget that third kiss!

When the evening summer heat subsided,
Mom opened the window.
Fresh air and the noise outside filled the room.
Maman sighed, "Since your father passed,
I felt all alone;
Today, with you on my side,
I felt important again."
Tears wiped away.

I watch Maman smile gleaming,
Friends and loved ones passing through,
Our walls fill up inside
With their known voices,

Meeting me again.
Two kisses from me.

An old man, aged by work under the sun,
Had once been a face my father knew;
With tears in his eyes,
And both hands on his heart,
I hear the knot in his throat,
"I miss him, your Baba-joon,
Welcome child, welcome."
This man did not sit in our home.
Instead he stood, out of respect for my father.
Tears flowed for Baba-joon.
They all came,
Wanting to catch a glimpse of his legacy.

Every morning, I woke up to the noise outside;
The aroma of freshly made bread,
Would fill my senses,
Satisfying my desire to belong.
Maman and I would sit at the same kitchen table.
The carvings of this old wooden table,
Heard many stories, many cries, and much laughter.
Cardamom infused tea would fill the air.
Familiar sight, Mom pouring tea from a Samovar.
At dawn, she shopped for fresh bread and figs.

She served home made jams;
"The orange blossom jam,
Your favorite."
"The blossoms from the orange tree of your father."

When Maman looked at me,
She saw the past.
With a longing to be part of a new story,
"And I bought you fresh figs,
Just like Dad used to bring you every morning."

Home is a memory.
My childhood a memory.
The noise of the street a memory.

At the breakfast table, an empty chair,
Filled with a ghost memory of my father.
I reach out,
Waiting to be held.
Cheek, cheek
And cheek again.

ಙ

The Heart of the Village

In the silence of pain,
I bear emotions
lost in the soul of the village
I left behind.
Emotions distilled into the bits of gravel,
In the majesty of the pecan trees.

Burned, out of deceit,
Sharing their silent stories
With the passing wind.
Lifeless homes left to defend themselves.

Lonely dogs wagging their tails,
Waiting, still, for the hail of their masters,
Wondering to where the glory disappeared?
Farmers go home at sunset,
After a long day of plowing;
They soothe their pain with remembering
The warmth of a welcoming eye,
The smell of a freshly made stew.
Stories told at dusk
By lanterns lit
With dissipated grandeur.
The heart of a village that once was.

Ziya-Cola was a symbol of who I was,
Who I have become,
The wisdom ingrained within every cell of my body,
A longing to be part of a heritage.

Ziya-Cola, the land of my ancestors,
The spirit of many hearts, many souls
Disappeared into the turbulence of life
In a war that was never won.

Ziya-Cola was more than my ancestral land,
It was my childhood.
Memories of laughter and mischief,
weddings and reunions;
New Year visits to Ziya-Cola
Was the highlight of my life;
Grandparents, great uncles & aunts,
Living in lonely homes,
Waiting every year for the first day of spring,
To celebrate a new year with family.
Lanterns lit brought life
To every corner of their homes.
The smell of spring cleaning,
And the freshly planted jasmine,
Filled the air.
We would all arrive the evening before, excited;
My cousins and I would wait at the gate
To welcome relatives arriving one by one.
"Uncle arrived from Tehran," we would announce,
Running to welcome each one.

I left Iran at seventeen;
Father insisted,
"Better education abroad." He told Mom,
An exaggerated illusion of life unknown!
Would I have left
if I knew he would be no more?

Or other loved ones would transition,
Some loudly and some gently, with the breeze?
Or if I knew the revenge of war?

Twenty-three long years later,
I am back with
My anguished heart
And missed opportunities.
What would life be like,
If I knew them better?
My body moved to stand up in the car,
As I entered Ziya-Cola,
A gesture I learned from Naneh-joon
"To honor the place,"
She told me when we visited Shiraz,
When I was fourteen.
The only time I travelled with her,
The first time I visited that Holy city.

Homes filled with life
Dot the new paved streets.
We turned the corner
To get to father's childhood home.
"Mom, I can't see it, where is it?"
She shrugged her shoulders!
Shoulders which carried all the burdens.

Ruins is what I saw;
Destruction of hearts, souls and homes.
I cried with my hands on my heart,
"They destroyed Agah-joon's home?"
"Out of revenge," Mom said.

"Grandpa was not one of them."
On the other side of the open field
was mother's childhood home.
"They burned my father's home,
my family still inside."
A shell remained.
I closed my eyes.
"I can't take it Mom,
I don't want to remember it this way.
I don't want to forget
How it used to be."

Memories flooded my mind …
The past majesty of our homes,
The warmth of my loving Naneh-joon,
Caressing me with all of her heart.
Playing with cousins in an open field,
Jumping fences,
Hiding from everyone,
Picking sticks in the cotton field,
Smoking cigarettes stolen from Agah-joon,
Dressing up in brand-new New Year's outfits,
Secretly taking freshly made sweets and Baklava
from Naneh-joon's kitchen,
Playing games in the evening
with all the family,
Singing our hearts out,
Laughing at jokes repeated over and over.

Everyone expecting Dad's practical joke,
Asking each other,
"What is he up to next?

Is he going to take the whole cooked lamb and hide it again?"

Ziya-Cola no longer exists for me.
What remains, is ancestral wisdom.
Every word of every story,
Lingers in the dusty air with the notes,
Of songs sung in the past.
Ziya-Cola no longer exists for me;
But stories are still alive,
Even in the graveyard.

ଔ

Naneh-Joon

"Nothing happens by chance,"
Naneh-Joon would say,
"We do not create our destiny,
The universe conspires to actualize our life."
A powerful presence,
Feisty in her ways,
Her big laughter drew you in,
And her stories captured us all.
"Each of us a flower growing in God's garden,"
"The perfume of our action is our alms to the world."
"Learn from the wolf of the desert,
Even they watch their back when hunting."
"Beware – actions have consequences."
Naneh-Joon taught me the lessons of life.
But nothing compared to how she lived her own,
With a surrendering heart
and reliance on ultimate Will,
The scent of her wisdom spread,
Low and high,
With no judgments.
Naneh-Joon would say,
"Life is a journey no one can predict.
Fate is in control of our destiny.
Wisdom comes as a token of His grace,
And grace as a token of our gratitude.
Pray, pray to be worthy of His grace!"

※

The relationship between my father and my grandfather, Agah Joon, was magical. My father held Agah Joon in high regard. Agah joon had a stately personality and many admired him. Dad, on the other hand, was down-to-earth. Everyone fell in love with my father's personality and was instantly at ease. They always found themselves laughing at his wonderful sense of humor.

During the Iranian revolution, religious intolerance and prejudice was at its height. Many people, including members of my family, were the target of attacks and were imprisoned because of their religious beliefs. My father, in order to save his own life, had to abandon his family and friends and live in hiding.

He eventually left Iran, leaving behind my mother, my sister and Agah Joon. He moved to another country and waited to get his paperwork so he could come to the US temporarily until it was safe to return to Iran. Hope of going back home diminished when the situation in Iran worsened. The emotional stress and his acute loneliness affected his health. After just a few months, Dad fell ill and tragically died at the age of 56, alone, with no close family around him. His death was a great loss to Agah Joon. Agah Joon was heard to say many times, "The only wish for a father is to leave this world before his beloved son. How can I move on with my life without feeling the kind of love he showed me?"

Grapevine Tree

Grandfather said, "If only I could."
His sigh broke my heart,
His pride hid his pain,
But I saw the pain in his smile,
And I saw the pain when he watched the sun set,
And I saw it in the way he picked grapes.

His fingers stretched out only halfway;
He stared at the grape and dropped it in a bucket,
Not paying attention as he used to
when he admired the shape of the grape,
When the color green had many shades,
When he smiled at the grape, plump and juicy,
When the grape was more than a grape.

He adored the sun for nourishing the tree.
He loved the rain for feeding the soil.
He loved the tree, the hands of his son planted.

Now he is tired,
His pain deep.
My dear grandfather lost his beloved son,
No hope, no love, no hate,
Just emptiness.
Longing for him in every moment.

Now lonely, he sighs,
Longing for the time he could love, again.

"If only I could see him one more time ...
I would kiss the hands that planted this tree,
The tree that brought me joy,
The tree that taught me love,
The tree that taught me to see with naked eyes.

"I would kiss those eyes that let me see.
I know I will learn to love again
For he showed me how."

ॐ

Don't Let Go of My Hand

The face of death,
I did not understand;
It was the end.
To part from you, was to be bare.
When you died,
I died with you.
How could I laugh again?
Or have hope?

But then, one sunny spring day,
Long after you left,
In my dream,
You came back to me,
With freshly picked jasmine in your arms.
"To understand life,
you need to understand death,"
You said with sparkles in your eyes,
The offering of jasmine
Suddenly in my hands,
I heard you say,
"With felicity embrace joy.
Happiness will fade like the scent of the jasmine,
But Joy will carry you through storms."
"This temporal life is transitory,
Immortality is being remembered,
For the fragrance you leave behind."

You took my hand,
 and I took my first step,
I looked into your eyes, I knew
You were never going to let go.

When you were alive,
You would come home late,
Tired and hungry, ready for rest.
Once I asked, "Please Baba-joon,
take me to the cinema."
Puzzled, with the same sparkle in your eyes,
You said, "Father and teenage daughter outing,
Have you gone mad?"
But, you never said no to me.
And with pride in my heart,
I walked fast behind you trying to catch up.

One night,
I was to study through the night,
You peeked into my room and whispered,
"I left it behind the couch."
I looked,
I beheld,
A treasure, behind the couch,
For no one, but me.
My favorite cream-filled Napoleon.
You always knew,
How to make my heart smile.

With the smell of those jasmine flowers,
I was gifted with the joy of your presence.
With your death, I was closer to you.
No façade, no pretense,
A symbol of eternal life.
Invoking all that you were within me,
Essence of Love.
Last night, before I closed my eyes,
With tears in my heart,
I asked again,
As I did so many other nights,
Baba-joon, are you with me?
From the depth of my heart I knew.
Yes. Always.

I open my heart to happiness and joy,
For you,
And for me.
But please,
Do not let go of my hand!

ೞ

Dreaming the dream

When I close my eyes
I see immensity.
I see a world beyond what I know.
I am transported to a magical place
Where pain and sorrows,
Hate and rancor are deceptions,
Where Beauty and Love,
Felicity and Bliss are the Breath of life.

-Felora Ziari

Dreams are gateways to an opening within us that is, normally, out of reach. Dreams can bring transformation once we are open to looking beyond material values. Dreams have always been my teacher, a source of inspiration and an opening to greater possibilities.

My dreams often flowed magically from my own subconscious as the world beyond spoke to my heart. They were a symbol of a magical world I knew existed but could not realize. One night, twenty years ago, I awoke from a vivid dream. I still remember all the details and can feel the emotions it caused. The experience was a turning point in my life.

In the dream, I stood at the edge of a cliff. I flew toward a mystical presence, arriving at a vast open space. I saw what appeared to be the Tree of Life. I knew that under that tree I would be able to meet the Divine, the Beloved. Hesitantly, with great exhilaration and fear, I moved toward the tree. Half way, I stopped to make sure I was ready to meet the Beloved. I took account of my inner and outer appearance and realized I was not ready. I had work to do and needed to turn back. I was disappointed, but I returned home, knowing what was missing within me.

The first thing that was missing had to do with unconditional love. I knew that, up until then, my love was given with the condition that I be loved in return. To love unconditionally comes easy for no one. But my heart knew that with this gift, this knowing of unconditional love, I would be 'ready' to return.

The other knowing was more difficult to embrace. I realized my happiness and my sense of belonging had been dependent on the things of this world and not on my inner being. I had to empty myself of the illusions of the material world so I could be filled with the wonders of the mystery.

The dream I had about my best friend on the night that she transitioned made me realize that all my life I have judged others. The false assumptions I made about them were based on fear. Each person I encounter has the potential to be a magnanimous teacher; I only need to "see" them for their true selves and their true worth. Because of that dream, my relationships had new possibilities.

Best Friend

When she left this mortal life too early,
It brought sadness and heavy hearts.
We shed tears for her missed opportunities.

I wished I could have known her better.
I never thought she would accept me as a friend.
I know she thought the same.
We were different in our choices of life's journey.
A label of our feeble mind!

The night of her passing,
She visited me in my dream.
The light of her beauty,
Delighted my heart
She smiled with great fondness,
She walked with humble stride.
Where was she going?
With my eyes, I followed her.
Admiring her stride, marveling her freedom.
My heart knew her destination,
The dwelling place of the Beloved.

In the dream, our souls connected;
A shift in my awareness,
No fear of rejection or judgment.;
The façade of mortal life was not a hindrance;
I saw her true essence and the radiant spirit.
The veil was lifted,
And I was revealed in her presence.

She lifted me up, conquering my fears.
She smiled knowingly,
And, since that night she never left;
She became my best friend!

The Mask of the Lion

When you believe, you will discern!
When you ask, you will receive!
When you are ready to know, the answers will come!
To perceive the truth is to have the wisdom to learn!
Dreams are windows to the worlds within,
A call to the vision of understanding.
One night, a dream set my heart free,
Discovering hidden gems.

I found myself in a beautiful garden,
Encapsulated by the blossoms of blooming trees,
With every breath, I took in the scents,
Roses, gardenias,
Earth.
My emotions were transformed;
I beheld all its essence.

A majestic lion appeared from beyond the trees;
The tranquility of the garden
interrupted with her presence.
Unaware of the consequences, I remained still.
Slowly, she clutched me
Before I could take my next breath,
the lion's embrace of power entwined with me,
And, in one movement, I was contained;
Held down, bound by my fears.

Her grip tightened;
No hope of deliverance;

My voice cemented in my throat.
I fled from the perfume of the garden
To seek help.
People walking around,
My agony invisible to them.
The fastened lion was veiled from their eyes.
No help could be offered.
Seeking refuge from my agony,
I came into another garden.

Deep in my despair,
I took charge of my own affair.
The lion, visible only to me,
Her paws held onto me.
Only I could release her clutches,
And her power over me,
One paw at a time.

Time passed slowly, as if paused by memory,
Until I pried off her last clenching paw.
She disappeared as if she never existed.
I woke up with a knowing in my heart;
My soul lifted from the abyss of a desperate cry.
Dreams free a mind constrained by false pretenses.

In my dream,
The serenity disrupted by power and control.
An external force merged with me,
Dominated my whole being.
Others oblivious of it's existence.
What was the true nature of the lion's grip?

From deep inside an inner voice cried,
"All the fears are veiled from others."
By loosening each paw of the lion,
I let go, one fear at a time;
Fear of inadequacy,
Fear of judgments,
Fear of defeat,
Fear of rejection!
Fear of not being good enough!
I had to see each, clearly,
One fear at a time,
And slowly unclench them from my heart.
With this, I rejoiced at the mercy
Of my perception;
I breathed in the pain, and,
With new found courage,
I breathed out the pain,
Releasing it to the unknown.
I was naked, my authentic self.

The illusion of old belief was no more.
Now I stood firm in my core,
No judgments.
No fear.
Without the mask of the lion,
I saw my noble self.

ଓ

WHISPERS FROM ABOVE

A Clearing Dream

Walking on the long bridge of life,
In the darkest hours of night,
The wind of destiny pushed me forward.
Nothingness above and below,
The ocean surging, I imagined.
Walking slowly at first,
Feeling my way out of the womb,
Then, faster.
Was freedom waiting for me?
Or was it nothingness?
As I got closer,
I shed the inner dialogues,
Emptied all thoughts,
Released all fears,
And arrived at the shore of an ocean,
Bare, with nothing to loose.

Warmth of the sand on my bare feet,
Fresh air embraced my whole being,
The sound of murmuring love caressed my ears,
And with nothingness inside,
I wailed the only words I knew
"He is the All-Glorious"
Over and over again.

My voice melodious.
I knew with this
In my heart,
On my tongue,

My wounds will be healed;
I did not need more knowledge.
I began to slowly shed
Unwelcome thoughts and emotions,
Bare,
Bare to the bone.
My sacred chants intensified,
Appeased the distant murmuring sounds.
Minds soothed.
Hearts humbled.
Doubts pacified.
The desire arose all around
To sing the same melody,
To witness the same Beauty.
In this moment of naked truth,
I arrived with open heart,
Dancing the tune of Universe,

ଔ

A woman's voice: a journey to inner beauty

Contradictions are the stories of our lives.
Who am I suppose to be?
A symbol of beauty or love,
A blade or a chalice,
A yin or a yang,
Or am I a soul that has no gender?

-Felora Ziari

Women have always felt the contradictions of what it means to be a woman. Our beauty has been celebrated and at times has been a curse. Our intuitive hearts brought us joy but, at times, have been interpreted as flaws. We have not been given the opportunities to completely embrace the right to celebrate who we are. In every country women learn that they must conceal their true selves behind masks of convention.

I grew up in a small town in the northern part of Iran where women lived on either side of a wall that separated the empowered from the powerless. Women on both sides of this virtual wall suffered from a duality of identity; they recognized, on some level, their true selves, but had to hide it, in some cases from their own selves.

Some women, like myself, lived in families that allowed them freedom of expression, but other families were fanatical in their beliefs, and held their women hostage to old standards. My family's faith tradition upheld the equality of gender; however, most of my friends grew up in families who adhered to the "old ways" and believed the woman's only role is in the home raising the children and caring for the family.

Once when I was a teenager, my entire family gathered around my grandfather to hear his stories of his recent trip to the United States. It was a day that changed my perception of my future. Grandfather told us stories of his travels and the beauty and modernity of the country. The room was full of people who could not imagine life outside of Iran. He told of how, in the USA, his strongest impression was that the people—all the people

—had freedom of expression—"Even women." I took that into my mind completely. I thought to myself. He told us that Americans are allowed to "live fully, see fully and feel fully." I have thought about his remarks for a long time.

I was awe-struck with his descriptions; I asked him, "Agha-joon, how can I manifest to "live fully, see fully and feel fully?" My grandfather looked at me and smiled knowingly and said, "Felora, one thing I learned travelling the world is that everything is possible, and I have no doubt that with your independent spirit and courage you will achieve whatever your heart desires."

My grandfather's validation of "Me" set me free to continually examine the masks that I put on myself. With his belief in me, I set out to prove I could achieve my heart's desire. First I became an engineer, a traditionally male role at the time, but I soon realized that this achievement was not a measure of my value. My true journey evolved as I strove to understand and advance the role of women in the world. I wanted to discern for myself how I could contribute to the world without the influences that hindered the generations who came before me. I remembered my dream as a teenager to live in a world that acknowledged my value as a human being—a value that was not based on my gender. My life, ever since, has been dedicated to the empowerment of women.

In this section "A Woman's Voice, A Journey to Inner Beauty," the poems are all for women who hope for the chance to truly use their voice with courage and grace.

Voice of Truth

If I am the bird of heaven,
Why this prison?
If I am free,
Why the confinements of oppression?

In my humility, I didn't use my voice.
In compassion, I devoured my needs.
In obligation, I said yes when my heart said no.

I am a woman who once had a dream.
I am a woman who once was a seeker.
I am a woman who once believed in herself.

I can't remember when my dreams faded away.
I can't remember where I buried my wishes.
I can't remember when I lost the girl within.

Life is a wheel of fortune,
Wherever it points, destiny lies.
Trusting in ultimate Will, hope lives.

One day, it could all come together!
The seeker within becomes the teacher.
Dreams become reality.
The girl within could blossom.
If only I could find the courage again,
to believe
in me!

The following poem is dedicated to a brave mother from a middle eastern country. During political upheaval and unrest, two of her young sons, who were only in their mid- 20's, were innocently charged and imprisoned. And, after few months of imprisonment, the authorities tragically killed them. Her only desire was to insure her beloved sons' lives were not lost in vain.

The Whispering Angel

She was the strength,
the kings have dreamt about!
She was the whispering angel
the poets wrote about!
She was the hero
the legends talked about!

At the peak of upheaval and unrest,
In the midst of war and hostility,
Seeking freedom for humanity,
Was a mother's revenge.
"The truth will set us free,"
She whispered
into the ears of her two sons
when taken away.
Ingrained in their soul
Was the voice of innocence,
Calling for freedom
From oppression,
For liberty,
For justice.

Then, one winter morning,
the revenge came as cold as the winter snow.
The streets turned red,
Souls died on either side.
Blood was shed.
In seeking freedom,
They lost their lives.

The mother stood proudly
at the pulpit shouting,
"If you loved my sons,

Clap your hands.
Beat the drums.
Celebrate their lives.
I gave up my sons
in a quest to unravel injustice.
Proudly they lost their lives only once.
Those who killed my sons
will die every single day of their life.
Justice will be done!
Their blood was shed so all could know the truth.
My sons gave only their blood,
The slayers gave their souls."

"O my loved ones,
Do not shed tears for my precious sons;
Dance and celebrate instead.
Tears of pain will bring pleasure to the tyrants;
Do not let the loss of the innocent be wasted.
Do not let it bring them satisfaction."

She bravely shouted,
"I am the mother of heroes!
I am the mother who embraced the cause of justice!"
Where are the mothers
of the aggressors deprived of Grace,
whose names will forever be lost
in a chapterless book?
I am the strength,
the kings dreamt about!
I am the whispering angel,
the poets wrote about!
I am the hero,
the legends talked about!

ॐ

FELORA ZIARI

The following poem was written in honor of my hero, Táhirih. Táhirih was an influential poet and an advocate for the emancipation of women in mid-1800's Iran. She lived during an era in which women were denied education, dominated by their families and did not have a voice. Táhirih was a beautiful, highly educated and very independent woman. She became a follower of a new religion and suffered a life-long opposition because of her new religion. She was one of the first women of her era that stood up for the emancipation of women. She advocated equality for women by breaking the Islamic practice of hijab. At a gathering, she removed her veil in the presence of men. This action caused such a great controversy amongst the men present at the gathering.

Táhirih was a legend in her own time. Despite the opposition from her own family, accusations by the clergy, arrests and imprisonment, she traveled extensively throughout Iran and neighboring countries advocating her message. In her mid- 30's, she was imprisoned for the last time and later martyred when she was strangled with a scarf that she gave her executioner with her own hands.

One of her most notable quotes is her final remark before her martyrdom: "You can kill me as soon as you like, but you cannot stop the emancipation of women."

Solace of the Eyes

"Solace of the Eyes" was her title;
The "Pure One" was her identity.
Táhirih was her name;
Remembrance of her hand is my remedy.

In the quiet moments,
When life takes its toll on me,
I feel her presence;
I am reminded of the essence of her mystery.
I open my hands to see the symbol of her love,
To find a place where all her strength lies.

With her right hand,
She wrote poems of hidden mystery.
She wrote of her unceasing search,
Her anguished heart to know,
Her desire to be with the Beloved.

With her left hand,
She gave away her scarf.
Wearing a white dress,
To walk the aisle of martyrdom.
To bravely claim her allegiance,
To leave the world behind and claim her true self,
To cleanse the world of misery,
To stand up for the emancipation of women,
And to free others by giving up her life.

She would lose nothing,
Only gain salvation for seekers of Light.
Freedom came easy to her.
They, who took her life, lost their hearts,
So Táhirih could live forever.

In the palm of my hand,
I beheld her mystery
For all to see, and
To open their own;
A great victory will be won.

Be a witness to her power.
Share her love.
Know her courage
For the Divine,
For which she gave her all.

ぞ

FELORA ZIARI

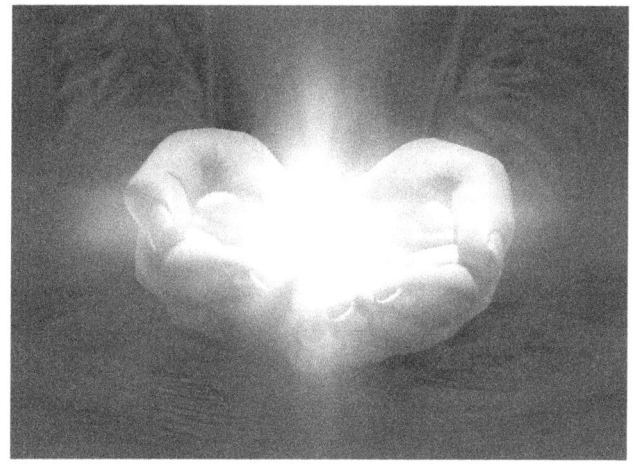

Do You Hear My Voice?

Will injustice ever be eradicated to give back your voice?
Will there ever be a day that the world could recognize the essence of your inner wisdom?
Will rancor and malice make way for equity and truth?

Vital is the feminine voice,
in uprooting hatred and dismay.
Crucial in planting the seed of compassion
in the womb of the world.
Prerequisite to the progress of humanity!

You stood proudly for generations
to abrogate the injustice.
You struggled all alone fighting for your rights.
You asked for the empathy and compassion you deserved.
You embarked on a frontier
to unlock the mystery of strength and courage.
You planted the seed of benevolence in the world.
From you, came children so powerful,
they ruled the world.
Nothing compares to the essence
of your nobility and wisdom.

Your courage set the world in motion.
Nothing can ever take that away from you!
When power made the unjust take away your honor,
Love made you have the courage
to teach them righteousness.

There will be a day when the world will stand up,
to honor all the women that were not given a chance.
There will be a day when the world will bow its head,
to salute the gift of motherhood.
There will be a day that your voice will be heard.
There will be a day that justice will prevail,
To give you a chance to claim your right!

ଔ

FELORA ZIARI

ABOUT THE AUTHOR

Felora Ziari was born in Shahi, Iran, and at seventeen moved to England to pursue an engineering degree at Oxford. Following graduation she embarked upon a sixteen-year career as an electro-mechanical project engineer and engineering management in the nuclear industry in the US. She left the private sector to dedicate her time to community service in the non-profit world that included her work in women empowerment, conflict resolution, dialogues through commerce, leadership and more.

Her passions for transformative action in women led her to establish and manage a non-profit platform called *ACT Women* in 1996. In the past few years, her consulting company, *Crimson Woman*, a leadership and human potential accelerator for women, organically came to fruition. Both organizations serve to enable people to transform their lives and achieve extraordinary results. She currently serves as a founding member of a global non-profit called *Peace Through Commerce Inc.*® for which she developed curriculum and led domestic and international workshops, striving for sustainable peace through entrepreneurial leadership and empowerment. Some of her recent work has taken her to Israel and Palestine where her collaborative efforts offered transformative tools to address deep-rooted perceptions between the multi-ethnic groups in these conflict zones.

In 2012 she was awarded a humanitarian award for her outstanding leadership contributions as board chair of Peace Through Commerce, United Nations Association and Interfaith Action of Central Texas (iACT).

Today she resides in Austin, Texas as she oversees her venture called Crimson Woman, a global platform for 360 transformative development for women. She is a speaker and consultant for cultivating leadership and maximizing human potential.

She can be reached through www.crimsonwoman.com.

Credits

Editing: Ron Frazer and Katherine Moore

Interior Design: Ron Frazer

Photos:

Back Cover	Swendner Photography
pg 1	Alexandra Lande/Shutterstock
pg 7	Tatiananna/Shutterstock
pg 15	Kletr/Shutterstock
pg 19	Transia Design/Shutterstock
pg 29	Rui Vale Sousa/Shutterstock
pg 33	Peter Waters/Shutterstock
pg 43	eva_mask/Shutterstock
pg 49	Meischke/Shutterstock
pg 53	Eugene Sergeev/Shutterstock
pg 61	Colorlife/Shutterstock
pg 77	Cranach/Shutterstock
pg 83	FPSO/Shutterstock
pg 89	LiliGraphie/Shutterstock
pg 97	Lina Balciunaite/Shutterstock
pg 101	Kosarev Alexander/Shutterstock
pg 123	romrf/Shutterstock

www.ingramcontent.com/pod-product-compliance
Lightning Source LLC
Chambersburg PA
CBHW031150160426
43193CB00008B/318